YouTube Jump-Start Guide for Small Business

Miles Austin

Copyright © 2013 Miles Austin

ISBN: 0989158705
ISBN-13: 978-0989158701

Published in the United States by Venture Road Publishing
(ventureroadpublishing.com)

Books in the New Tools for Business Series are available at special discounts for
bulk purchases for event promotions, trade associations or team use. Special
editions, including personalized covers, excerpts or compilations of other books in
the series can be created in large quantities for special needs. For more information
email **specialmarkets@fillthefunnel.com**

DEDICATION

To everyone that has the courage, passion and vision to start your own business. You are on the journey of a lifetime. Best wishes.

CONTENTS

ACKNOWLEDGMENTS

Thanks to Dora Austin, my Mom and role-model for my entire life. Her persistence, patience and devout faith in God have guided me throughout my life. May she rest in peace.

NEW TOOLS FOR BUSINESS SERIES

As I travel and speak to audiences throughout North America, I have the privilege of meeting business people of all type ranging from Fortune 100 executives, a start-up founder whose company is still in her kitchen, and everything in between. Over the past year or so, I have been asking everyone how they prefer to learn these new technologies and tools. Do you prefer to read a 300 page book with everything is covered? Would you prefer audio or video formats for learning these things? How about electronic versions for Kindle or your tablet app? The overwhelming majority answered no to the above questions.

What they told me was that they wanted something with a specific focus, on a specific tool, in print, so that they could write notes, highlight and add sticky notes for those things that were important to remember or reference. Many said that they have a bookshelf full of business books that are 300+ pages and they never finish them. I asked why and they said that they didn't have the time to read it through and they just got discouraged when they were not able to complete the book.

It was as a result of these comments and responses from them all that guided me to create this series of step-by-step guides I call "New Tools For Business". My goal with this series is to provide you with concise, step-by-step guides to get your business up and running on these new tools and approaches to growing and running your business.

When you are ready to tackle Twitter, you can grab the Twitter Jump-Start Guide for Small Business. When video is on your to-do list, YouTube JumpStart Guide for Small Business is ready for you. Exactly what you need, when you need it, in a print version ready for you to use the way you prefer to implement these new tools.

I hope you like this approach and that I will be able to support and guide you through the maze of new business tools and thinking.

I encourage you to visit **www.newtoolsforbusiness.com** to select from the growing list of titles available in the series. While there, read the blog to learn about how these tools are being used in businesses around the world.

Make sure that you sign up for our email service, to allow us to send you updates on new titles as they are released, webinars and seminars on these topics in your area, and special promotions, bundles and checklists that we offer from time to time.

1 - INTRODUCTION

Are you using YouTube for any of your content marketing right now?

If not, consider these statistics for a minute:

➢ More than 1 billion unique visitors to YouTube every month
➢ Each month, more than 6 billion hours of video is watched
➢ 100 hours of video are uploaded each minute
➢ YouTube reaches more adults aged 18-34 than any cable network
➢ Every second there are approximately 49,296 videos being viewed around the world

….and

YouTube is the second largest search engine, right behind Google.

Even better, your YouTube videos will show up in Google search results. In effect, you get traffic both from YouTube and Google for the same small effort.

So, what's stopping you?

For many people, it's just a matter of taking the first small steps to break through your hesitance and fear of what's involved.

This is easy, cheap, effective marketing that can reap huge results for your business. People aren't looking for glitzy, slick videos on YouTube. You can quickly put together a 3 minute screencast or "Top Tips" video and have it up on YouTube in minutes.

In this guide, you're going to go through each of the basic steps of getting started on YouTube……right from the first step of setting up an account.

We won't be teaching you how to create video – that's for another day. However, you will learn how to upload one and do some basic editing.

Let's get started!

2 - SETUP YOUR ACCOUNT

Sign Up

We'll start by setting up your YouTube account.

1. Go to www.youtube.com

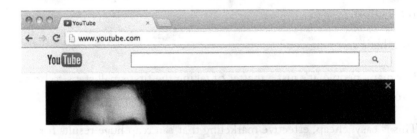

Click 'Sign In' in the top right hand corner.

2. Click 'Create an Account' in the top right hand corner.

3. Input all of the required information. Use a strong password.

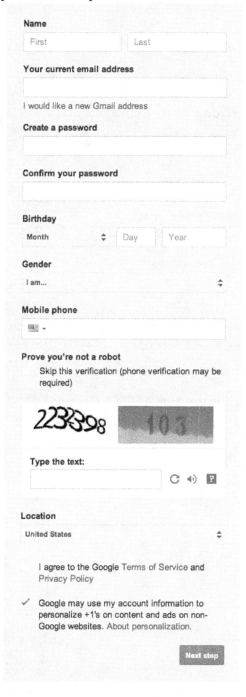

Verify your Account

4. Verify your account by entering the verification code that was sent to your phone. This should have only taken a few minutes to receive. If for some reason you haven't received yours, click the 'Try again' button beneath the input box.

5. Verify your email address by clicking the link in the email that was sent to you. This, again, should only take a few minutes to receive.

Get Started

6. In the page that pops up from that link, add a profile photo to your account. Click 'Next Step' when you're done.

7. Click 'Back to YouTube' to return to the main page.

Set up a channel

8. Click on your profile image in the top right hand corner to bring down the drop down menu. In this area you will find most things that you will need when using YouTube.

9. Click on 'My Channel' in the drop down menu.

10. Click 'Ok' on the screen that appears to create a channel using your name… or alternatively, follow the link to use YouTube as a business or another name.

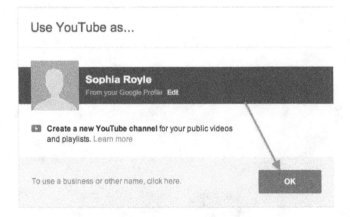

3 – UPLOAD YOUR VIDEO TO YOUTUBE

1. Click 'Upload' in the menu bar at the top of the screen.

2. Click the icon in the center of the video upload box to select the video you'd like to upload from your computer. Select 'Choose' to begin the upload. Alternatively, use the icons to the right of the screen to create a video using your webcam; create a slideshow or a Google Hangout broadcast.

3. In the upload screen, you will see the video upload progress at the top. Enter the relevant information for your video – Give it a description and enter some relevant 'Tags', or keywords that describe the content of the video. Toggle the privacy setting if you don't want your video to go public just yet, and make sure you give it a relevant category so the Google can list it in the correct area.

When you give your video a description, be sure to include a link to related content that you'd like people to visit, especially if you're using the video to promote another website or product. Try putting the link at the very top of the description, and be sure to test it.

Tagging

In order to give your video the best chance of being seen by as many users as possible, you need to make sure that the Tags are as relevant and definitive as possible. A tag needs to define the video at it's most primary and objective level… so if you've uploaded a video of a dog for example, you'll need to tag that as 'dog' and 'animal', not 'video of a dog'.

If you have a brand name, make sure you tag it in different variations; for example 'brand name' and 'brand name'.

YouTube itself will offer some good tag suggestions, so pay attention to what they recommend. You can also take a look for existing content that is similar to your own to see what other people have tagged – this might give you some good ideas.

If you are creating a series of videos, try to use at least one tag that relates to the name of the series so that people can easily find the other videos in that series.

4. Once your video has finished uploading, you can view it by clicking on the link given at the top of the page.

5. You can use the icons at the bottom of the video to view the statistics and settings, make some enhancements such as filters or add captions to your video.

4 – EMBED A VIDEO INTO A BLOG POST

YouTube shouldn't be the only place you put your video. You should embed it into your own blog, as well as encourage others to do the same. You can certainly embed other people's videos too, and both YouTube and WordPress make that easy.

1. Once you've uploaded your video to YouTube, copy the URL found in the address bar of the video page.

2. Simply paste the video directly into your post under the 'Visual' tab.

3. Make sure the link you've pasted is NOT a hyperlink. To remove a hyperlink, click the button in the editor's menu.

4. WordPress will automatically insert your video with a standard size. In order to change these sizes, you just need to use a 'shortcode'.

To turn your link into a short code you need to use the following format;

[youtube=YOURLINK**]**

…so it would look a little something like this…

[youtube=http://www.youtube.com/watch?v=Xl65O425FK0]

Notice that the only alteration you need to make to your link is to add 'youtube=' to the front of it, and to use square brackets either side.

In order to alter the dimensions, you need to use a little more shortcode. The width of the video is defined by the code '&w=…' and the height is defined by '&h=…'; the sizes you need must be added immediately after the = in each instance.

This code must be added directly after the link, within the square brackets… so it should look something like this...

[youtube=http://www.youtube.com/watch?v=Xl65O425FK0 **&w=640&h=385**]

You can use any size in replacement of the 640 x 385 used in the example above.

5 – EDIT YOUR VIDEO

YouTube has its own powerful editing features that many people don't take advantage of. That alone gives you an advantage over a large portion of your competitors. None of the editing features are difficult to use, and all you need to do is explore and experiment a bit to get the hang of it.

1. Go to the dropdown menu found by clicking on your profile icon in the top right hand corner.

2. Click on 'Video Manager'.

3. In your video list, click the 'Edit' button next to the video you'd like to work with.

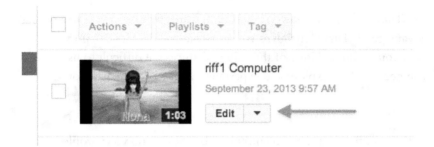

4. On the next screen you can see the information about your video, such as the file type, how many times it's been viewed and likes and dislikes.

Using the images to the right of the video, you can choose another thumbnail that will be shown to viewers.

Here you can also alter the title and description of the video.

Custom Thumbnails

Once your account has been verified and in good standing with YouTube, you can upload a custom thumbnail. It is recommended that you take advantage of this ability when you have it... the opportunity to use whatever you wish is a great one as it's the thumbnail that visitors first see. A good thumbnail can mean the difference between someone skipping over your video or having it grab their attention.

If you do have the ability to upload your own thumbnails, you will find it directly beneath the three YouTube suggested ones.

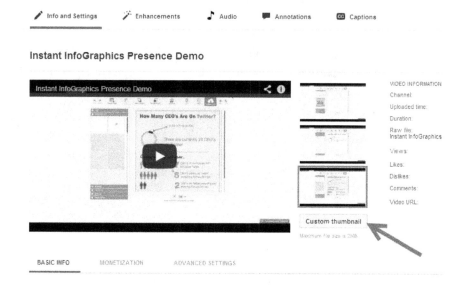

In order to get the perfect thumbnail, remember the following points;

➢ **Relevance**. We all know cats are popular on YouTube… but resist the urge to use the photo of one just to get clicks. You'll end up with a bunch of unhappy viewers who feel like they've been deceived into watching your video. If your video is about lasagna; make sure there's lasagna in the thumbnail.

➢ **Where possible, use content from the video**. If your video is of a high quality, grab a good still shot from it and use that. You're telling people exactly what they're going to see.

➢ **Use Text**. A little text on the thumbnail will again immediately tell people what they're about to see. Use some image editing software to write your title or key point on your thumbnail. A great free online image editor is http://pixlr.com/. Remember that it's not a huge image so make sure it's easy to read!

➢ **Make it eye catching**. You're competing against A LOT of other content, so making yours stand out as much as possible is incredibly important. Use bold colors, for example, to attract the eye.

➢ **16:9** YouTube thumbnails use a ratio of 16:9 – make sure your image adheres to this to avoid getting a squished thumbnail. You can use a free online ratio calculator such as www.bmyers.com/public/2144.cfm to figure this out.

Let's continue on with more editing options.

5. Click on 'Enhancements' in the top menu bar. Click on any of the images to the right of the screen to add a filter to your video. You will see a split screen on the video itself so you can see the original and newer version of the video at the same time.

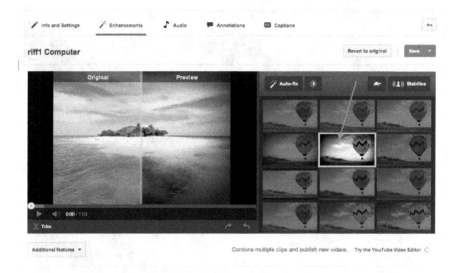

6. Using the 'Trim' button at the bottom left hand corner of the video itself, you can alter where the videos begins and ends.

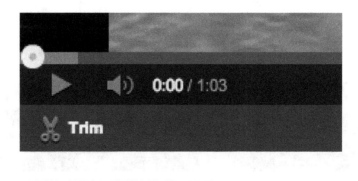

Simply drag the bars either side to where you want the beginning and end, and click 'Done' when you're finished.

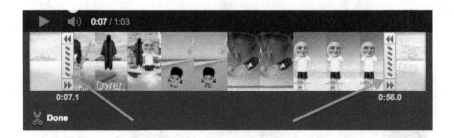

7. Clicking the 'Auto Fix' button to the right of the screen will automatically 'fix' lighting and color in your video.

8. You can manually adjust the contrast, saturation and other color fields using the 'Fine tuning lighting and color' button next to the 'Auto Fix' button.

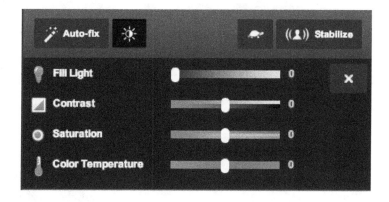

9. To slow down the video, click on the 'Slow Motion' button to the right. Here you can select if you want the video to run at 1x, 2x, 4x or 8x speed.

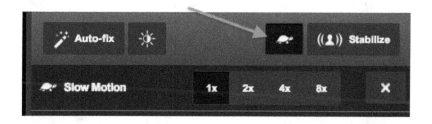

10. Click on the 'Stabilize' button to remove any shaky camera movements in the video.

11. Remember to click 'Save' to keep any changes you've made!

12. Click on the 'Audio' tab in the menu bar to change the audio. You can select any of the tracks seen to the right of the screen, or search for something specific.

    Click 'Save' to keep changes.

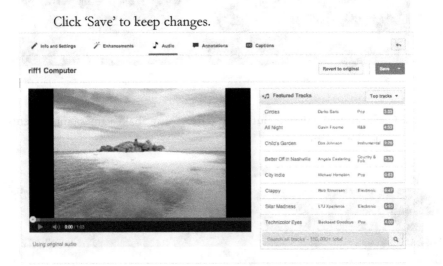

13. Click on the 'Annotations' tab to add comments to certain parts of your video.

Drag the slider on the timeline underneath the video to select a certain time, and then click 'Add Annotation' on the right. Select the annotation type.

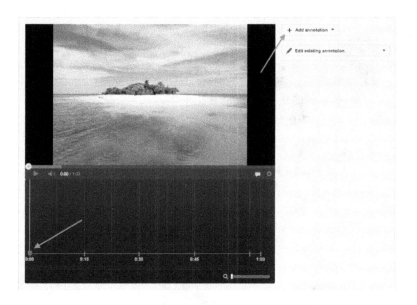

14. Add the text you'd like to include and edit it using the editor's buttons below. You can change size, color, etc. Select the 'Start' and 'End' times.

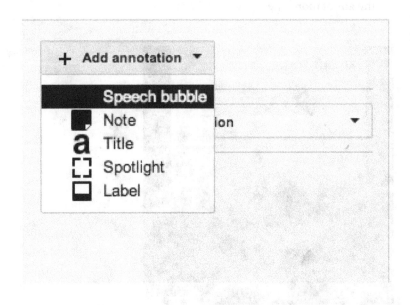

Annotations

Annotations are a fantastic tool to not only engage and communicate with viewers, but also add any extra information that you have missed within your video.

You can add links to other videos in your annotations easily – when adding your annotation, simply check the 'link' box and then include the video link. You can edit the starting point of the video and select whether or not you'd like the window to open in a new window – which is recommended so your viewer doesn't lose what they were initially watching.

When writing annotations, there are some key points to remember.

➤ Keep the distraction down to a minimum. Don't leave your annotations on for too long a period of time; you don't want to take too much emphasis away from your video. A good rule of thumb is to keep them between 5 & 7 seconds.

➢ Use as little space as possible. You don't want to cover any important parts of the video.

➢ Use vibrant colors to make them stand out.

➢ Position them to the borders of the screen. Again, avoid covering any important aspects of your video.

➢ Don't overload your video. Keep your points specific and to a minimum.

Lastly, for the editing options, let's take a look at captions and transcription.

15. Click on the 'Captions' tab on the menu bar to add captions to your video. In this screen, click the 'Add Caption' button.

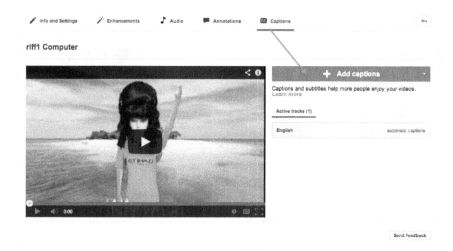

16. Here you can 'Transcribe and sync' captions, or upload an existing file. To transcribe and sync, click the option in the drop down menu.

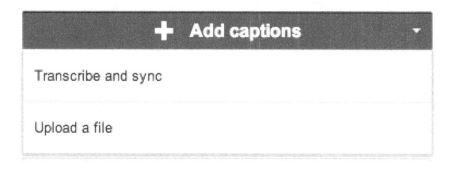

17. Type the video transcript in the box provided and click sync to add it to the video.

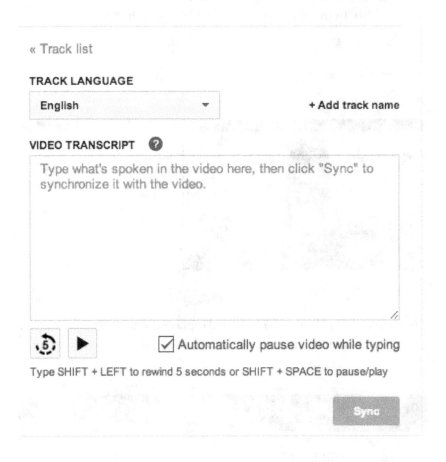

If you can take the time to add transcriptions to your video, YouTube will love you, but don't let it stop you from moving ahead.

With any of the video editing options listed here, you can always go back to your old videos and edit them, add annotations, captions, etc. Just get that video up there for starters.

6 - Create a Playlist

Playlists are a great way to make it easy for your visitor to watch several related videos at once. You can make a series of short, related videos that people can sit back and watch – one after the other.

Playlists are also another separate listing on YouTube and can show up in search results, along with the individual videos themselves. And you only need two videos to make a playlist!

1. Go to the video page you'd like to add to your playlist. This can be one of your videos, or any existing videos on YouTube.

Beneath the video player, you will see 'Add To' – click this to open the playlist window.

2. To create a new playlist, simply enter a new playlist name in the box provided and click 'Create Playlist'. Toggle the privacy settings where appropriate.

3.

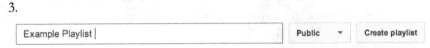

4. You'll then see that your new playlist, along with the amount of videos listed in it will appear in the playlist window. The videos within it are shown in brackets, i.e. (1).

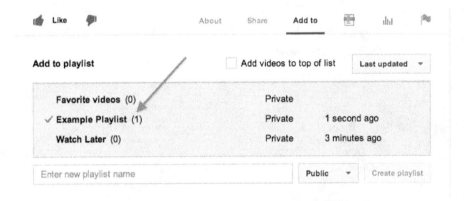

5. To add another video, go to the video page, click 'Add To' and select the appropriate playlist.

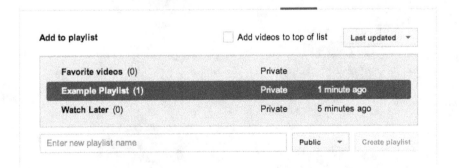

6. If you already have a number of videos, or even just two, that you want to put in a playlist, you can do this from your Video Manager just by checking off the boxes next to each video you want in your playlist. Then click on "Add to New Playlist" and fill in the details.

7. To edit your playlist, click on the drop down menu from your profile icon and select 'Video Manager'.

8. To the left of the screen, find 'Playlists' in the menu.

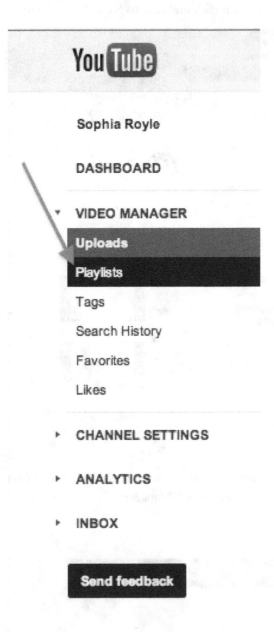

9. Click 'Edit' to the right of the playlist that you want to edit.

10. Give your playlist a brief description. This will help greatly for people who want to find content such as yours.

11. You can add a note to a video by clicking the 'Add a Note' icon to the right of the video thumbnail.

12. You can also adjust the Start and End time of each video by clicking on its respective icon. This is a great tool if your playlist is specifically focused on one topic and you have extra content in some of the videos.

In the window that appears, simply drag each bar to the desired beginning and end of the video.

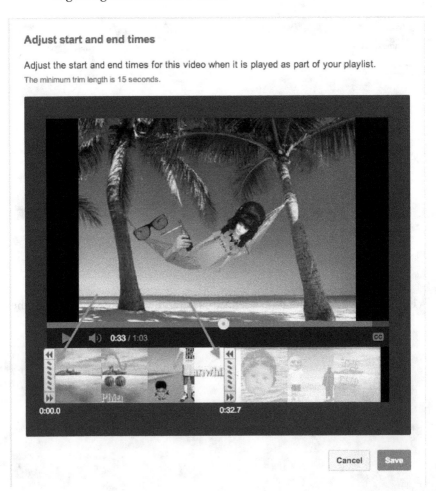

13. Selecting the video, you can add tags to it, or remove it from the playlist.

10 TIPS FOR YOUTUBE MARKETING

1. Keep your video short.

People generally have small attention spans and the percentage of viewers that are going to stick around for your big finale - and link information - after even 5 minutes is pretty slim. Ty and keep your information brief and to the point. Use your YouTube channel as a method of enticing viewers to view your other content, and give them more information when they get to that point.

2. Don't forget about your mobile audience.

A growing number of people are using their phones to access YouTube and watch videos. Bear that in mind when you're including text – it has to be easily viewable on a small screen.

3. Watermark your content.

Keep your information secure and not easily reproduced by others by adding a watermark to your video. Just make sure it's not too overpowering that it distracts from your content.

4. Spread the word.

Having a consistent level of communication between your YouTube, Twitter, Facebook and other social media accounts will do wonders for your flow of traffic. As soon as you've produced a new video, get it out there and let everyone in your network know about it. The good news is that it will automatically post to your Google+ account since you'll already have your Google and YouTube accounts linked.

5. Focus on SEO.

Add captions, tag your content, add a succinct description, think hard about your title and make sure your video file name is relevant, (dog-chases-car as opposed to 10-10-13) ... these are all great methods of making sure your content gets viewed.

6. Think about Audio.

You want to make sure your audience is engaged... but not overwhelmed. If you have spoken audio, it's good to include intro and outro music to the video. YouTube has some fantastic options to choose from.

7. Prepare your videos.

Use the best quality video and audio equipment as you can afford right now. Keep shaky camera movements to a minimum and plan the video before you shoot it – think about writing a script and practice first!

8. Link.

Make sure you take good advantage of the fact that someone is viewing your content – give them a link to the rest of your content or relevant content, and make it easily accessible in both the annotations and the video description.

9. Do something different.

Never has 'thinking outside of the box' been so important. You're up against a lot of competition and the more you stand out, the better.

10. **Go beyond YouTube.**

Once you've created your video content there are plenty of other video sharing sites online where you can post it and increase your audience.

CONCLUSION

At this point, you've learned how to:

> - Create your YouTube account
> - Upload your first video
> - Do some minor editing
> - Create a playlist
> - Start employing some best practices

You have no more excuses for NOT using YouTube, except that you now might be worried about how you're actually going to create a video to upload!

The trick is to just start with something...anything.

Try one of these options, picking whichever sounds easiest to you:

1. Create 5 PowerPoint slides with your Top 5 Tips for [something that will help your viewers]. Then hook up your microphone and click on the "Record Slideshow" option in PowerPoint and talk through the slideshow. When you're done, just save it as a video (only works with PowerPoint 2010 and above). You could also use a screen capture tool such as Camtasia to record the slides and your voice as you go through.

2. Outline a short task that you do on your computer regularly and which other people might not know. It could be as simple as dragging a file into an email, or inserting a table into a document. Then fire up a screen capture software and record yourself doing that task. Jing is a free program you can use that captures videos less than 3 minutes which is a good length.

3. Do you have a digital camera or a webcam? Write down 3 questions people have asked or might ask about your business. Then record

yourself talking through the answers. You could also do this on slides and add some images if you want.

These are just a few simple, quick ways to get some experience sharing your message with the world through YouTube. Your second effort will be better than the first, and your third will be better than the second. Jump in and just start creating your videos and sharing your message on YouTube.

Jump Start Guide for YouTube Checklist

Set Up Your YouTube Account	
Done?	**Task**
	Sign up with YouTube
	Verify your account
	Set up a Channel
Upload a Video	
Done?	**Task**
	Go to the 'Upload' page and select your video file to upload, or drag and drop it into the upload area
	Add a captivating, enticing title for your video
	Add a Description (don't forget to add a hyperlink!)
	Add Tags (keywords for people to find your video)
	Select your categories

Embed a Video into a Blog Post	
Done?	**Task**
	Copy the URL of your video
	Paste it into your blog post
	Use Shortcodes to alter the size of your video player

Edit Your Video	
Done?	**Task**
	Go to the 'Edit' page for your video
	Change the thumbnail, or add a custom one if possible
	Add a filter to your video
	Change the start and end points of your video with the 'Trim' function
	Fix the lighting and color of your video with the 'AutoFix' function

	Adjust the contrast and other color fields using the 'Fine tuning' function
	Adjust the speed of your video using the 'Slow motion' function
	Use the 'Stabilize' function to remove any camera shake
	Hit 'Save' to keep any changes you've made
	Add annotations to your video using the 'Annotation' function
	Add Captions to your video

Create a Playlist

Done?	Task
	Locate the video page you'd like to add and click 'Add To'
	Create a new playlist
	Go to another video page and add it to the playlist you've just created
	Find the Playlist section under your video manager menu

	Go to the 'Edit' page and enter a Description for your playlist
	Add a note to your playlist
	Alter the start and end points of a video in your playlist
	Add tags to a video

You can download a printable copy of this checklist at:

www.newtoolsforbusiness.com/youtubechecklist

ABOUT THE AUTHOR

Miles Austin is known world-wide as "The Web Tools Guy" through his work at FilltheFunnel.com. He has a 30 year history in tech sales and management with international, regional and local companies including NYNEX, CompuCom, and Dell amongst others. He has started three of his own companies in tech and consulting, having sold his previous two companies prior to Fill the Funnel. Miles writes about, speaks, trains and consults with companies of all sizes about how to take advantage of the internet and the software and hardware that are now available to businesses of any size. Recognizing early on the possibilities that social media platforms and tools possess, he brings his readers and audiences the most up to date thinking and ideas on using these powerful tools for the improvement of business owners everywhere.

Miles currently lives in North Bend, WA.

You can learn more about Miles and his work by visiting www.fillthefunnel.com or emailing him at maustin@fillthefunnel.com

Twitter: @milesaustin

www.ingramcontent.com/pod-product-compliance
Lightning Source LLC
Chambersburg PA
CBHW061042050326
40689CB00012B/2932